Create and Share   Thinking Digitally

Researching with Online Videos

By Kristin Fontichiaro

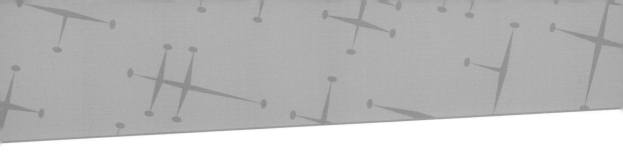

CHERRY LAKE PRESS

Published in the United States of America by Cherry Lake Publishing Group
Ann Arbor, Michigan
www.cherrylakepublishing.com

Series Adviser: Kristin Fontichiaro
Reading Adviser: Marla Conn, MS, Ed., Literacy specialist, Read-Ability, Inc.
Book Designer: Felicia Macheske
Character Illustrator: Rachael McLean

Photo Credits: © Howard Klaaste/Shutterstock.com, 5; © Master1305/Shutterstock.com, 6; © myboys.me/Shutterstock.com, 9; © LightField Studios/Shutterstock.com, 19

Graphics Credits Throughout: © the simple surface/Shutterstock.com; © Diana Rich/Shutterstock.com; © lemony/Shutterstock.com; © CojoMoxon/Shutterstock.com; © IreneArt/Shutterstock.com; © Artefficient/Shutterstock.com; © Marie Nimrichterova/Shutterstock.com; © Svetolk/Shutterstock.com; © EV-DA/Shutterstock.com; © briddy/Shutterstock.com; © Mix3r/Shutterstock.com

Cherry Lake Press is an imprint of Cherry Lake Publishing Group.

Library of Congress Cataloging-in-Publication Data has been filed and is available at catalog.loc.gov

Cherry Lake Publishing Group would like to acknowledge the work of the Partnership for 21st Century Learning, a Network of Battelle for Kids. Please visit *http://www.battelleforkids.org/networks/p21* for more information.

Printed in the United States of America
Corporate Graphics

Table of
CONTENTS

CHAPTER ONE
Using Video for Research 4

CHAPTER TWO
Searching 8

CHAPTER THREE
Finding What You Need Quickly 12

CHAPTER FOUR
Being a Savvy Video Researcher 16

GLOSSARY 22
FOR MORE INFORMATION 23
INDEX 24
ABOUT THE AUTHOR 24

Using Video for Research

An adult needs help fixing the leaky sink. Your friend wants to know how to sew something on her jean jacket. Your teacher just said, "We're going to do a research project." When you need to learn something, where do you go first? A lot of people enjoy learning from videos on websites like YouTube.

Watching a video and *learning* from it are different. As you watch, you need to listen and look for detailed information. You'll need to listen for sounds that teach you something. This book will give you **strategies** for learning as much as you can from videos.

Watching a how-to video is sometimes easier than reading instructions.

Learn a new dance by watching a step-by-step video.

ACTIVITY

Different Ways to Learn Something

Pick something new to learn. Maybe it's a dance to a song or juggling. Perhaps you really want to learn how to wrap a gift well. Then search online for step-by-step instructions. Search for three different types of instructions. One type should use text only. Another type should use text and pictures. The third type should use video. Which type of instructions do you think would be the easiest to learn from? Test it out! Were you right?

CHAPTER TWO

Searching

When you search for a video, you need to think about the words you will type in the search box. If you don't know, you'll have to make your best guess.

You're at home with your dad when you both hear *drip, drip, drip*. Uh-oh. The sink is leaking again! You grab your laptop to look up a video on how to fix it. But you're not quite sure what words to use. So you go to YouTube and guess, "leaky sink."

Before you finish typing the words, YouTube provides suggestions under the search box. So, you pick a phrase that sounds better than what you could have guessed. It's "leaky sink basket strainer: most common leak."

Narrow down your search results by using filters.

Now you have hundreds of possible videos to choose from! Which one should you visit first?

You could just start at the top of the list and keep watching videos. You could watch them one after another, until you find the one that matches the problem. But one of the top videos is 17 minutes long!

There's a better way. If you don't know much about the topic, it is helpful to watch a short video first. This quickly shows you the tools you may need. It may also give you the **vocabulary** to describe the problem. If that doesn't answer your question, you can always watch another video. Then you haven't wasted much time.

To find short videos, look for the Filter button under the search box. Under Duration, pick Short. Some have numbers like 3:41 or 2:37 in the video box. This describes how long the video lasts: 3 minutes and 41 seconds, or 2 minutes and 37 seconds. Scroll through the results. Read the descriptions. Then choose a video to start your research.

ACTIVITY

Learning Something New

You got a yo-yo for your birthday. You want to learn how to do the "Around the World" trick with it. What words would you use to search for the trick? Type the words into YouTube. Can you find a good video that explains it in 3 minutes or less?

CHAPTER THREE

Finding What You Need Quickly

Remember that your sink is still leaking. You need answers in a hurry! Luckily, YouTube will let you decide the playback speed, or how fast the video will play. **Hover** your mouse on the video. Click on the settings icon, or the wheel gear, at the lower right-hand side of the video. Click Playback Speed. Choose any number above Normal to slow down the video. To speed up the video, choose any number below it. Anything faster than 1.5 speed will probably be too difficult to understand.

Some YouTube videos have ads. Look for Skip Ads in the bottom-right corner if you have the choice. Don't forget, the sink is still dripping! You start playing the video. But even going at 1.5 speed, the introduction is taking a long time.

Want to skip past the introduction? Hover the mouse over the video. See the line that is red and gray? That's the **timeline**. The red shows you how far into the video you've watched. The gray shows you how much of the video has **buffered**.

Hover the mouse over the bar. A small **still image** of the video should pop up. Trace the mouse over the line. You'll see the still image change. This can help you skip the introduction and go directly to the part you want to watch. Just click the spot on the timeline to start the video there.

Using these time-saving techniques, you can move quickly from one video to another until you find the one with the answers you need. Success! Together, you and your dad stop the leak and save the kitchen from becoming a wet mess!

I CAN'T SEE THAT FROM HERE!

Your dad is under the sink. He wants to watch how to move the wrench in a tight space. You need to make the video screen big enough for him to see.

Below the timeline, click on the box icon to the far right. It will make the video fill the whole screen. Now your dad can see without wriggling out from under the sink!

Beyond YouTube

YouTube is the world's most popular video site. If your school blocks it, try these sites instead. Vimeo is a lot like YouTube. SchoolTube and TeacherTube have videos made by students and teachers about school topics. Search a topic at Google or Bing. When you get the results, click Videos under the search box. You'll find videos from around the web.

CHAPTER FOUR

Being a Savvy Video Researcher

Imagine you're working on a research project about the arctic fox and its habitats. Your research question is, "How do arctic foxes change their body or their behavior to adjust to their habitat?"

You started your research the way the librarian suggested. You read an encyclopedia entry and got some basic facts. Now you need to see what the animal looks like and how it moves in its natural habitat. This will help you answer the research question. Watching a video would definitely help!

Don't always speed up the video. The video sound might sound off or weird if played too slowly or too quickly. Play the video at normal speed first to get the most information. You can always pause or go back whenever you need to.

Turn on closed captions. Sites like YouTube want everybody to understand what is being said. This includes people who cannot hear. YouTube's computer **algorithms** turn the speech in videos into words shown on-screen. If you turn on **closed captions**, you can see the text as words are said out loud. You can find this option at the lower left side of the video. It's the icon with "cc." The algorithm does make mistakes. But seeing at least some of the words can increase your understanding.

Use full screen. When you are watching videos to learn, you want to see all the details and not be distracted. Set it to full screen.

Use headphones or earbuds. Sometimes, videos don't have high-quality sound. Headphones or earbuds can help you block out outside noise and hear more clearly.

Watch the video more than once. To answer the research question, you need to do three things. Watch how the arctic fox moves. Listen to what it sounds like in its habitat. And hear the **narrator** describe what is going on. Watching the video at least twice will help you catch everything.

Make notes. When you hear or see something useful, write it down in just a few words. It's okay to click pause so you can write something down.

What will you learn next?

Timestamp your notes. When make a note, look for the timer that shows how far into the video you are. Write down the time. This **timestamping** will help you find the information again if needed.

Now you know some tips to help you learn all you can from videos!

CITE THIS

When you do research for class, your teacher or librarian might ask you to cite your source. That means telling people where your information came from. Cut-and-paste the title, creator, and URL of the video into your notes. This information will also help you find the video again in the future.

Can You Kendama?

Kendama is a Japanese toy made of a stick and a ball. People learn tricks to throw and catch the ball on the stick. Go to http://bit.ly/kendama-video to learn how. Watch the video and make notes. Pause when you need extra writing time. You might even have to slow down the video! Now read your notes to a friend. How good were your notes? Did you write down too much? Not enough? Or just what you needed?

GLOSSARY

algorithms (AL-guh-rith-umz) actions a computer follows to complete a task

buffered (BUHF-urd) loaded or processed on the internet

cite (SITE) to write down where your information came from

closed captions (KLOHZD KAP-shuhnz) a feature that lets people see the text of what is being said in a video

hover (HUHV-ur) to hang over or rest on top of something

narrator (NAR-ay-tur) the person who explains things in a story or video

still image (STIL IM-ij) a non-moving picture

strategies (STRAT-ih-jeez) tips and ideas for how to do things

timeline (TIME-line) a bar underneath your video that shows how much has already played

timestamping (TIME-stamp-ing) labeling your notes with the time you learned them in the video

URL (YOO AR EL) stands for uniform resource locator; it is the "address" you type into a browser to find a web page

vocabulary (voh-KAB-yuh-ler-ee) a word or words that are explained or defined

BOOKS

Moening, Kate. *Susan Wojcicki: CEO of YouTube*. Minneapolis, MN: Bellwether, 2020.

Owings, Lisa. *YouTube*. Minneapolis, MN: Checkerboard, 2017.

WEBSITES

SchoolTube
SchoolTube.com
Watch educational school videos on many subjects posted by teachers and students.

TeacherTube
TeacherTube.com
Find a huge variety of educational videos posted by teachers for students.

INDEX

ads, 12

Bing, 15
buffering, 13

captions, closed, 17
citations, 20
closed captions, 17

earbuds, 18

filters, 9, 11
full screen option, 18

Google, 15

headphones, 18
how-to videos, 5

images, still, 13

learning, 4, 7

notes, 18, 20

playback speed, 12–13, 17

research, 4–7

SchoolTube, 15
searching, 8–11, 12–15
sound, 17, 18
sources, citing, 20
step-by-step videos, 6, 7
still images, 13

TeacherTube, 15
time-saving techniques,
   12–14
timeline, 13
timestamps, 20

URLs, 20

videos
   playback speed, 12–13, 17
   searching for, 8–11
   smart researching, 16–21
   time-saving techniques,
      12–14
   using for research, 4–7
Vimeo, 15

YouTube, 4, 8, 11, 12, 15, 17

About the AUTHOR

Kristin Fontichiaro teaches at the University of Michigan School of Information and writes books for adults and kids.